official

buppie*
handbook

*Black Urban Professional

by
Thayer William Staples, IV
and
Katherine McMillan Staples

PYRAMID DESIGNS PRESS
Pittsburgh • Pennsylvania

An Original Pyramid Designs Press Paperback
Copyright © 1985 by Pyramid Designs Ltd.

All rights reserved. No part of this book may be used or reproduced in any manner whatsoever without written permission from the Publisher.

Pyramid Designs Ltd.
Pyramid Designs Press
1017 Investment Building
Pittsburgh, Pennsylvania 15222

Printed in the United States of America

Library of Congress Catalog Card Number 86-60080
ISBN 0-937071-00-5

> Pyramid Designs Press books are available at special quantity discounts for bulk purchases for sales promotions, premiums or fund raising. Special books or book excerpts can also be created to fit specific needs.
>
> For details write Pyramid Designs Press, 1017 Investment Building, 239 Fourth Avenue, Pittsburgh, Pennsylvania 15222. Attention: Special Markets (412) 642-6698.

Contents

Introduction 1

Chapter One ... The Buppie "Look" 7

Chapter Two ... The Buppie "Ride" 13

Chapter Three ... The Buppie Education . 17

Chapter Four ... The Buppie Family 21

Chapter Five ... The Buppie Home 27

Chapter Six ... The Buppie Vacation 33

Chapter Seven ... The Buppie Diet 37

Chapter Eight ... Buppies into Athletics and Fitness 43

Chapter Nine ... Buppie Singles 47

Chapter Ten ... Buppie Entertainment ... 55

Chapter Eleven ... Buppie Careers 61

Chapter Twelve ... Buppie Finances 69

Chapter Thirteen ... The B*aaa*d Buppie . 75

Final Observations 81

INTRODUCTION

The Official Buppie Handbook is a tongue-in-cheek look at black people who have managed to get . . . and hold on to, a piece of the American Dream. There are obvious similarities to the Yuppie (Young [and white] Urban Professional) culture. Both groups tend to have excellent academic credentials from prestigious universities, good jobs and salaries, and a passion for acquiring the best of everything — clothes, cars, homes, furnishings . . . and outside of possessions, enjoying the best restaurants, sports facilities, vacation spots . . . .

However, contrary to the pronouncements in the white media Buppies are *not* "Yuppies in blackface." Buppies do not need white role models — they strive out of historical circumstance, not out of a need to imitate whites. They are striving for a better life not simply as a means to an end, but as a matter of black pride and development. It's now "okay" to try for the "good life" . . . and the Handbook allows Buppies to take a few moments out from hectic schedules to smile at themselves.

You are a Buppie if you are between the ages of twenty-five and forty-five (give or take a few . . . or more than a few if you *really* want to identify with this phenomenon) AND want to "get ahead," "make it," and achieve the American dream AND . . . .

One: The Buppie "Look"

"THE BUPPIE LOOK"

- You most definitely "dress for success."

- You have the basic (male) wardrobe: a two-color, polyester and wool single breasted plaid suit; at least two good pin stripes; a tan summer poplin suit in polyester and cotton; a navy blazer; a 3/4 length trench coat with belt, epaulets, etc.; a cardigan vest with Fair Isle trim; (banker's striped) cotton shirts; regimental striped silk ties and leather kilties with tassels.

- You wear Hickey-Freeman's Boardroom collection, Hart Schaffner & Marx and Austin Reed ... and of course, Harris Tweeds.

- You never go to work or formal occasions without your Rolex.

- You have your initials on your dress (work) shirt.

- You wear Ballys, Allen Edmonds, Stacy Adams or Johnston & Murphys shoes.

- It goes without saying that your 'gators are most definitely the genuine article.

- You "week-end" in Perry Ellis and Alexander Julian sweaters.

- Your gold filled Cross pen is on the upper end of their price scale.

- You have a gold signet ring.

- You have an ostrich leather carry-on for short trips.

- You are "definitely into" Investment Dressing and buy your clothes accordingly.

- You have the basic (female) wardrobe: a black linen suit and a light colored silk suit; an "unconstructed" tweed blazer; a classic (Investment Dressers are into classics) constructed oversized blazer (preferably red); a long plaid skirt; a two-piece neutral dress to "mix 'n match"; neutral colored blouses in silk and crepe de chine; dark and light slacks; dress sweaters (some with sleeves "as alternatives to jackets"); an all-weather coat with detachable lining; simple gold jewelry; leather bags, leather belts, leather gloves and leather shoes.

- You have a "working wardrobe" of Liz Claiborne, Harvé Bernard, Anne Klein, and similar labels.

- You own at least two designer jogging suits, one in Gore-tex.

- You wear one tasteful gold wrist chain with your watch.

- Your snakeskin shoes are real . . . you wouldn't think of buying cheap imitations.

- You occasionally use tinted contact lenses to change your "look".

- You tried a "curly" hairstyle but are now returning to the "relaxed" look.

    . . . or you have a superbly trimmed, incredibly neat and sculptured

natural... usually worn with a lot of "tastefully applied" make-up and dramatic earrings.

- You have the beginnings of an ultra suede collection.

- You buy "black" AND "white" cosmetics (for example, Ultra Sheen AND Maybelline!)

- You wear the Michael Jordan "athletic shoe" (a.k.a. sneaker).

- You have a wig but it's made of a fiber that resembles the texture of black hair and is not "wiggy" looking... only for going out at night... for a change.

- You like the long skirts, flats, matching stockings, baggy pants, etc... but would buy a leather miniskirt for fun.

- Your closet also has touches of Vittadini, Willi Smith and Kenzo — for "something different."

Two: The Buppie "Ride"

THE BUPPIE "RIDE"

- You and your spouse are aspiring Buppies with one car and a cutesy license plate like "KEV-KAR" for Kevin and Karen.

- You and your spouse have matched personalized license plates like "HIS" and "HERS".

- You think a Cadillac is "très gauche."

- You know a Saab costs as much as a BMW . . . but you're stuck on the "ultimate driving machine."

- Single Buppies still favor a long, sleek (preferably red, white or black) Corvette.

- You are content with your BMW for now, but you really want a Porsche and your wife really wants a Mercedes. (On the other hand if you already own the Porsche and the Benz, you've reached ultimate status in Buppiedom!) See Chapter 13.

- ... but you still "check out" the Lincoln Continental every year.

- It goes without saying that you have a tape deck (Dolby Sound) and a state-of-the-art radar detector. You're fond of speeding in the rain in your Porsche to pass eighteen-wheelers (and incidentally, other cars) to show off how well it hugs the road.

- You have a telephone in your car.

- You picture yourself as a sporty old dude with a Jag.

Three: The Buppie Education

THE BUPPIE EDUCATION

- You graduated from a predominantly black college but always quickly point out that your Master's, Ph.D., J.D., M.D., etc. is from Harvard, Yale, Princeton, Duke, or some other prestigious white institution.

- You are a product of Boston's massive intellectual community — Harvard, Northeastern, B.U., M.I.T., etc.

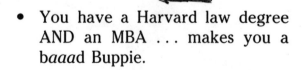

- You have a Harvard law degree AND an MBA ... makes you a b*aaa*d Buppie.

- You know it's not a matter of IF your kid(s) will go to college ... just where.

- Your toddler is enrolled in a private, integrated, international, preparatory, educational preschool.

- Your kids are enrolled in private schools whose names start with "THE (as in "THE _ _ _ _ SCHOOL), and/or end in "DAY SCHOOL" or "INSTITUTE" or "ACADEMY".

- You send consumer-oriented complaint letters to the president of the company and "cc" it to the regional director, local store manager and the salesman who sold you the defective goods . . . all by certified mail, of course.

- Your son attends a military academy.

- You actually use the word "eclectic" in conversation . . . if you're single, it's to describe the decor in your apartment.

- You can use the phrase "très gauche" in a sentence.

Four: The Buppie Family

THE BUPPIE FAMILY

- You attended Lamaze classes with your wife and assisted at the birth of your child.

- You have one child and will seriously debate whether or not to have another one.

- Your daughter's name is Megan, Ashley, Blair, Alexis, Melissa, Jennifer, Mikki, Tiffany . . .

- Your son's name has III, IV, or (even!) V after it; alternatively it is Michael, Theodore, Eric, Chad, Taylor, Geoffrey . . .

- Your kids are signed up for dance, acting and music ("creative arts") classes, including piano, Suzuki or voice; computer literacy and beginning tennis or golf.

- You got "whippins" but you are teaching your children "to coOPerate."

- Your kids always attend a two week sleep-away camp in the summer which includes a program of backpacking, canoeing, horseback riding, tennis and soccer.

- Your kids belong to Jack 'n Jill to "stay in touch" with black folks.

- Your daughter is actually "coming out" in a cotillion . . . because the proceeds go to a black "cause" or her school's scholarship fund.

- Your teenager wears deck ("boat") shoes and a back pack to school.

- You and your spouse really do share the household chores equally as you pursue your separate careers.

- You have your family tree traced and recorded on a flow chart.

- You have a retriever . . . Golden or Labrador will do.

Five: The Buppie Home

THE BUPPIE HOME

- You are renovating a town house in a neighborhood that used to be called a ghetto but now is made up of "fashionable row houses."

- Your water softener "conditions" your entire water supply ... not just in the kitchen.

- You have purchased authentic African art work to decorate your home.

- You have a matching set of oak furniture for your infant's nursery.

- You have ceiling-high flourishing greenery in several spots in your house or apartment.

- You have household help in at least once a week.

- You own a condo or are a part owner in a cooperative.

- You have a classic Spode pattern as well as a contemporary geometric design for everyday use.

- Your home computer was IN your home long before media hype made it "in".

- Your (one) child has a small brass bed ... to match your own.

- You live in an area of "gracious older homes."

- You like art deco but reject it in order to make an investment in more traditional decor ... unless you're single.

- You have a library with an oak desk, banker's lamp and leather furniture.

- You have a modem on your home computer to tap into various "on line" services.

- When shopping for your home you were concerned about "architectural details."

- Levolors are okay for the child's room and home office but custom made drapes are an absolute requisite for the living and dining rooms.

- If you're single your art deco decor is gray and mauve . . . or white and silver.

- You have SOME kind of unusual collection: porcelain owls, old comic books, silver Christmas tree ornaments, electric trains, etc.

- Your neighborhood has antique shops AND ethnic restaurants.

- You have a hot tub or Jacuzzi AND a pool.

- You have a fairly elaborate security system to protect your valuables.

- You have at least three clock radios, two portable telephones, a telephone answering machine, a 35mm camera, a Polaroid, a complete stereo component set (see Chapter 10), a movie camera, several calculators, an intercom system, numerous kitchen gadgets (see chapter 7), and several televisions including one HUMONGOUS color Curtis Mathes in the living room.

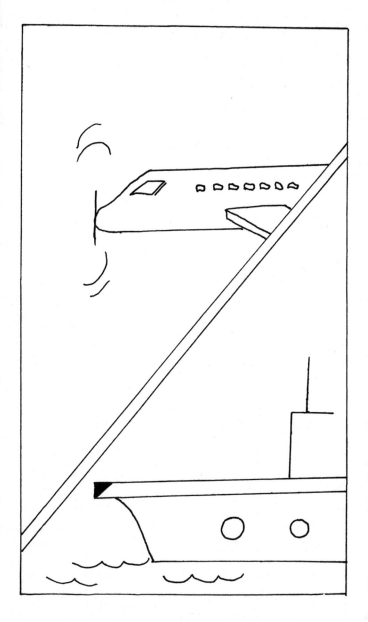

Six: The Buppie Vacation

THE BUPPIE VACATION

- It's a given that you've been to the Bahamas ... probably while you were in college.

- You wouldn't think of going to the Caribbean in the summer ... unless it was a long week-end jaunt.

- You are part of that special group of black folks that spend a few weeks each summer "on the Cape" —usually at Martha's Vineyard.

- You've been to Cancun at least once.

- Your family has been to Disneyland at least twice.

- You've already been to Paris and London and are planning for Rio de Janeiro the next time around.

- You've actually been white-water rafting ... and not only survived, but LIKED it.

- You own a timeshare vacation unit in Florida.

- You are planning a trip to the Far East.

- You make frequent trips to St. Thomas to take advantage of the tremendous shopping bargains.

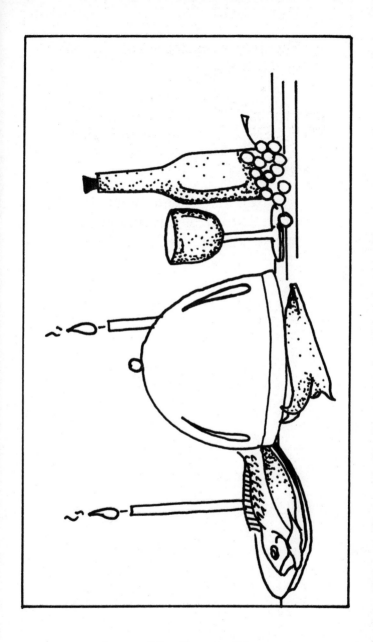

Seven: The Buppie Diet

THE BUPPIE DIET

- You call your refrigerator "the fridge."

- You have a variety of gadgets in your kitchen: microwave oven, electric corn popper, electric juice extractor, food processor, electric pasta machine, electric barbecue grill, ice cream maker and assorted cordless rechargeables...to name a few.

- Although not a vegetarian, you pay close attention to the amount of red meat you consume in any given week.

- You are a purist about your coffee and only buy Columbian roast.

- You furthermore only order Expresso in a restaurant.

- You like to cook and have taken the time to develop a knack for Creole and Cajun cookery which you love to show off to friends when entertaining.

- Your "everyday" ice cream is Haagen-Dazs and you regularly keep two to three different kinds in the "fridge."

- You shop in a gourmet delicatessen for delicacies for the weekend bar-b-que.

- You average three business lunches per week.

- You eat lunch at a fashionable restaurant/deli in town and would not be caught dead with a brown bag from HOME.

- You use the services of a "gourmet take-out" to avoid cooking at least twice a week.

- You carry a calorie-counter book in your purse and write down everything you eat.

- Your fridge always has Perrier (the way others keep ginger ale on hand).

- You know it LOOKS pretty in a bowl because its pink ... but you also know it's cold, it's made from beets, cucumbers, garlic, milk and sour cream and you're NOT gonna eat any cold pink borscht!

- You still enjoy collard greens and black-eyed peas ... and have a good laugh when you see them in the Yuppie delis as "delicacies."

**Eight: Buppies Into
Athletics and Fitness**

BUPPIES INTO ATHLETICS AND FITNESS

- You firmly believe in "no pain, no gain."

- If you really do like to ski (not a sport that attracts a big black clientele) you do it vigorously, hit all the good slopes, etc. . . . that is, you don't pretend by sitting around the fire at the lodge. You've been to Stratton and Stowe and/or Aspen and Vail.

- You've given up smoking to improve your performance; if not, you're trying to cut back.

- You play tennis, golf, racquetball, or chess (or some combination thereof) and teach your kids to play.

- You "shoot hoops" only in a fitness club gym (just to keep the white boys "lined up") . . . not on the local playground.

- You belong to a fitness club/spa and "firm up" regularly on the Naulilus equipment.

- Your wife is in a "Jazzercise" class.

- You wear a designer leotard to your exercise class (with coordinated tights and leg warmers . . . in contrasting colors, of course) at a local fashionable health spa.

- You own (and actually carry with you on business trips) a portable total-body exercise system. If you USE it, you can move to the B*aaa*d Buppie catagory. (See chapter 13).

- You have some serious exercise equipment in your home . . . and not only use it but have special space set aside for it.

- You have season tickets to a major pro team's home games.

- You rise early to exercise before heading to work . . . always arriving by 8 o'clock A.M.

Nine: Buppie Singles

BUPPIE SINGLES

- Your "man" or your "woman" is now called your "partner."

- You can really identify with the "where you're going, it's Michelob" commercial.

- You respond to the question of future plans with "a family (of two to three children), a successful career, and intellectual and personal development." (The number of children is reduced to one after you get married.)

- You do not believe that "something is better than nothing" and therefore do not tolerate dishonesty in your "partner".

- If you are a single parent, you scrupulously keep your social life separate from your child until you are certain your partner is ready to treat your child in an appropriate manner. ("Appropriate" is up to the individual.)

- You subscribe to Essence AND Cosmopolitan; Black Enterprise AND GQ.

- You are prepared, on a moment's notice, to pack a picnic lunch of cheese, pepperoni sausage, fruit, croissants and a rose wine for you and your Buppie man (... er, ah ... partner.)

- You have "platonic" friendships with members of the opposite sex with whom (you emphasize to your partner) you are NOT sexually involved.

- You usually answer "What are your interests?" with "jogging, tennis and reading" or "piano, astronomy and backpacking" or "travel, jazz and good restaurants" or "dance, theater and good films", etc.

- You pride yourself on NOT suffering from I'll-Never-Find-Another-Man disease and pursue your own interests, hobbies, career, etc.

- You have attempted an African dish at a social gathering more than once.

- You are committed to your career, and right now, do not want to be "involved" . . . and make no apologies for it.

- You are struggling with the new "sexual etiquette": should I just come right out and ask, "Have you now or have you ever had VD?" . . . or not?

- "All" you are looking for is a relationship based on honesty, trust, consideration, respect, open communications, and a shared view of the world.

- You attend at least one or two social-conventions-masquerading-as-"professional development seminars" per year.

- If you and your partner are living together you probably:
    a) have a combined income of at least $50,000
    b) share expenses and keep meticulous records
    c) are ignoring your partner's hints (or pleading) to get married
    d) pretend to be very liberal and open about relationships but privately go into jealous rages if the other person gets too attentive to someone of the opposite sex at a party.

Ten: Buppie Entertainment

BUPPIE ENTERTAINMENT

- You eat out at least twice a week . . . and we're not talkin' Micky D's here!

- You prefer a concert of Wynton Marsalis to an evening in a stadium with Kool and the Gang.

- You like Denzel Washington and discuss his powerful performances on television and in the movies at social gatherings.

- Your kids have at least five different kinds of electronic games.

- You prefer a good Cabernet Sauvignon or Chardonnay

- You are "into" Fusion music

- You'd rather drink a California Cooler than Beefeaters or Cutty Sark . . . but you also like Chambord, liqueurs, and B & B.

- You never miss the Ebony Fashion Fair when it hits your city.

- You actually do stop at your favorite bar after work for "Miller time".

- You do occasionally attend the symphony, the opera, a (black) repertory company or the ballet. You may even subscribe . . . to one of the above.

- You prefer a Heineken to a common local "brew".

- Your kids always have some sort of catered birthday party.

- You keep California "sparkling wines" on hand for summer get-togethers.

- You make "a weekend of it" in New York (or other major city) to catch the Alvin Ailey Dance Theatre.

- Your stereo system includes AM/FM stereo cassette recorder, graphic equalizer, ultralight headphones, auto reverse, high speed dubbing, automatic program selection system and Dolby sound.

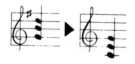

Eleven: Buppie Careers

BUPPIE CAREERS

- You believe you know how to "monitor the climate" in your office and play the corporate game.

- You work in the Silicon Valley . . . in management, of course, unless you are one of those entrepreneurs with your own firm.

- You belong to the National (professional) Association (bar, dental, pharmaceutical, etc.) AND its white counterpart.

- You work in the management track for one of the following corporations: GTE, Control Data, Digital, Raytheon, Honeywell, RCA, Procter & Gamble, Pitney Bowes, McDonnell Douglas, Lockheed, Hewlett-Packard, Bechtel, Phillips Petroleum, Grumman, Lever Brothers, Shell, A.B. Dick, Burroughs, Stewart-Warner, Black & Decker, the Coca-Cola company . . . or

- one of the diversified financial companies such as American Express, CIGNA, Transamerica . . . or

- You are in management in marketing, advertising, corporate sales, land development, securities transactions, banking, or music production.

- You work on Route 128 in and around Boston.

- You are part of management in one of the major banks such as Citicorp, BankAmerica, Chase Manhattan, Manufacturers Hanover, J.P. Morgan, Chemical New York, Security Pacific, First Interstate, Bankers Trust New York, First Chicago, Mellon, etc.

- Your company regularly sends you to "career development" seminars.

- You have thoroughly read at least one career guide book and regularly skim others in the book store.

- You have "consultant" on your business card.

- You are "networking" and developing relationships with "mentors."

- You are with one of the major investment bankers: Merrill Lynch, Goldman Sachs, First Boston, Salomon Brothers, Morgan Stanley, Stearson Lehman Brothers, Drexel Burnham Lambert, Bear Stearns, Paine Webber or E.F. Hutton.

- You resent supervision which you view as "hampering your creativity."

- You have "specialist" or "analyst" or "representative" or "planner" at the end of your job title (as in business systems specialist, budget analyst, marketing representative or financial planner.)

- You've read at least one "management strategies" book in the last year.

- You think community service is important too ... and it usually takes the form of fraternity/sorority activities; Big Brother/Sister programs; tutorial centers; sports clinics; or lending your expertise to minority groups.

- You work in one of the office park centers in Northern Virginia (e.g. McLean, Vienna, Reston, Tyson's Corner) or in Montgomery County in southern Maryland.

- You LOVE "vis-a-vis" and (over) use it in the office every chance you get.

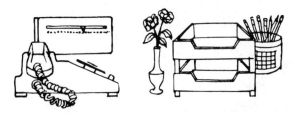

- You are a doctor, lawyer, architect, accountant (especially CPAs), television newscaster, professor, lawyer, engineer (civil, electrical, mechanical, industrial, chemical, aeronautical, petroleum or nuclear!); an editor, an insurance agent regularly in the Million Dollar Round Table Club, an entrepreneur grossing more than a million dollars AND operating in the black (no pun intended), or a successful entertainer ... Buppie membership is automatic.

- You belong to one of the airlines' "frequent traveler" bonus programs.

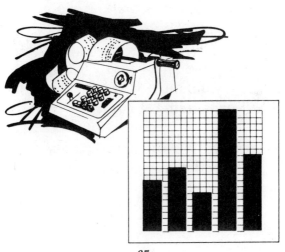

- You are one of the new "young wizards" (or potential wizard anyway) in the management phases of telecommunications, computer science and electronics.

- You own and are running your own business . . . a B*aaa*d Buppie (see Chapter 13) has his own office in the heart of downtown.

  . . . or you work for one of the major insurance companies such as Prudential, Metropolitan, Equitable Life, Aetna, New York Life, John Hancock, Travelers, Connecticut General, etc. . .

  . . . or one of the major retailers such as Sears, K-Mart, JC Penneys, Montgomery Ward, Macy's. . .

  . . . or one of the major transportation companies or utilities . . . all in management, of course.

- You work in the Research Triangle Park in the Raleigh-Durham area of North Carolina.

Twelve: Buppie Finances

BUPPIE FINANCES

- Your major topic of conversation is the latest on "financial planning."

- You give to the United Negro College Fund every year.

- You subscribe to an investment newsletter and the Wall Street Journal.

- You have a savings plan in effect for your toddler's college education.

- You've been to at least one (rather costly) all day seminar offering financial advice and have attended a few of the real estate investment seminars ("Own your own home with no money down!)

- You have been looking for a "venture capitalist" for a great idea you have for a business . . . but would settle for a small piece of a UDAG grant.

- You have a Gold MasterCard with a minimum $5,000 limit.

- It is a given that you have an IRA . . . and have had one since they first became available.

- You belong to an investment club.

- You are investing in any combination of the following: stocks, bonds, money market funds, mutual funds, T-bills, IRAs or real estate.

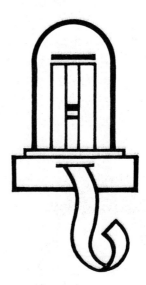

- You have a substantial amount in a high yield money market account.

- You not only know what a MESBIC is, but you have sought help from one for a "venture" of your own.

- You are buying an apartment house for "investment income".

- You have an investment portfolio which you deem to be "properly diversified."

- You and your spouse actually sit in the family room after the child has gone to bed and discuss how you can achieve "financial independence."

Thirteen: The B*aaa*d Buppie

THE *BAAAD* BUPPIE

- You never go out without your Rolex watch ... period.

- You really prefer to shop for clothes in Europe because you feel the styles are three years ahead of the United States.

- You not only attended the birth of your child ... you took pictures.

- Your daughter's name is Alexandra, Marissa ... or Sloan. Your son's name is Thatcher ... or Howell.

- You used the services of an interior decorator in choosing the furnishings for your home.

- Your wardrobe is 100% ... 100% silk, 100% cotton and 100% wool ... polyester is a foreign word.

- Your oven has a grill *and* rotisserie.

- You have "choice property" in a "prime vacation spot" for "investment income."

- You imported your car (cars) from Europe.

- You own a brand new (preferably red) Porsche 944.

- You have a trainer come to your home for a personalized physical fitness work-out.

- You regularly go to a professional masseur to relieve the tension which results from on-the-job stress.

- Your kids have had riding and sailing lessons.

- You ask for the sommelier upon entering a fine restaurant.

- You have had cosmetic surgery for purely cosmetic reasons.

- You've invested in a condo at Hilton Head.

- You patronize polo matches.

- You are debt-free and use only your American Express card . . . its limit need not be stated.

- Your child has a Clifford Trust . . . which you are looking into because recent tax cases may put its financial advantages in jeopardy.

- You have an investment bank AND a commercial bank.

- You own a home on the Cape.

- You have access to corporate aircraft.

- You and your spouse have matching Rolex watches.

- You actually need the telephone in your car to conduct your business.

- You enjoy horseback riding on the beach at your "summer place."

- Your company flies you from city to city as a "troubleshooter."

- You've moved your checking and saving accounts into higher yielding NOW accounts.

- You not only have your own business, you are a manufacturer and have your own plant.

- You have a horrendous monthly dry cleaning bill.

- Your kids have substantial Uniform Gift to Minors Accounts and/or zero coupon Treasury bonds.

- You have a preference between Haagen-Dazs and Frusen Gladje.

- Your business has a Dun & Bradstreet rating.

- You own a powerboat . . . as well as ALL of the other accouterments of Buppieness.

- An annual cruise is a given.

BON VOYAGE

FINAL OBSERVATIONS

We do not want the reader to think a Buppie's entire existence revolves around "conspicuous consumption." We note Buppies are in a unique position to help the vast majority of black people who do not enjoy the fruits of financial independence.

We believe that if you are a Buppie, by and large
- You still attend and/or support your church, and maintain strong ties with your communities, alma maters, civil rights organizations and (extended) families.

We all owe a debt to *some*one. Let us not let education, money, position, possessions and the lifestyle that results from these things allow us to forget "from whence we came."

TWS, IV
KMS

SEE **YOUR** "BUPPIENESS" IN PRINT.

Did we leave out some part of YOUR "look," "ride," education, family, etc??

Send your Buppieness to the address below and see it published in "Buppies - Part II"!!

Pyramid Designs Press
1017 Investment Building
239 Fourth Avenue
Pittsburgh, Pennsylvania 15222

Flaunt Your Buppieness!! Order your Buppie TEE-Shirt, Buppie Ladies Tote Bag, Buppie Key Chain and the Buppie Mug. Get a copy of the handbook for your friends. All items have Buppie logo.

Buppie Tee-Shirt . . . . $ 15.00
Buppie Ladies Tote . . . . $ 12.95
Buppie Key Chain . . . . $ 5.50
Buppie Mug . . . . $ 7.50
Buppie Handbook . . . . $ 4.95

Pyramid Designs Press
1017 Investment Bldg., 239 Fourth Ave.
Pittsburgh, Pennsylvania 15222

(412) 642-6698

(order form on next page)

Order Blank

Date _____

Name _____
(please print clearly)
Address_____
City-State-Zip _____
Telephone No. (_____)_____
(so we may call if necessary concerning your order)

____Check or Money Order Enclosed

****

| Quantity | Item | Size (XL,LG,MD,SM)* | PRICE |

_____
_____
_____
_____
_____
_____

*Indicate "C" for Children's Sizes

Total Amount for all items: $ _____
PA. Residents add 6% sales tax: $ _____
Shipping and Handling: $ _____
Total Invoice Due: $ _____

Please allow 2-4 weeks for delivery.

Shipping Charge   **Schedule**

up to $25.00 ....$ 2.00
$25.00 to $40.00 ....$ 3.00
$45.00 to $75.00 ....$ 5.00
$80.00 to $100.00 ....$ 7.00
$100 ....FREE!!

Order Blank

Date _____

Name _____
(please print clearly)
Address_____

City-State-Zip _____

Telephone No._____
(so we may call if necessary concerning your order)

____Check or Money Order Enclosed

****

Quantity   Item   Size (XL,LG,MD,SM)*   PRICE

_____
_____
_____
_____
_____
_____

*Indicate "C" for Children's Sizes

Total Amount for all items: $ _____

PA. Residents add 6% sales tax: $ _____

Shipping and Handling: $ _____

Total Invoice Due: $ _____

Please allow 2-4 weeks for delivery.

Shipping Charge   Schedule

up to $25.00 ....$ 2.00
$25.00 to $40.00 ....$ 3.00
$45.00 to $75.00 ....$ 5.00
$80.00 to $100.00 ....$ 7.00
$100 ....FREE!!

1. Close, neat natural
2. Relaxed hair
3. Foulard print
4. Leather bag
5. Silk Suit
6. Jazzercise shoes being used to save wear and tear on leather dress pumps
7. Johnston & Murphys
8. B*aaa*d leather briefcase
9. Rolex watch (never flaunted)
10. Pin stripe suit
11. Silk tie
12. 100% cotton shirt

NOTES:

NOTES: